MW01243329

This Journal Belong To:

This Journal Belong To: